The Seven Mindsets Of Highly Effective Teachers

Become a better teacher today

By

Tom Czaban

First Published: September 2016

Cowboy Press LLC

Table of Contents

Introduction 1

Mindset 1 4

Mindset 2 12

Mindset 3 22

Mindset 4 31

Mindset 5 40

Mindset 6 46

Mindset 7 54

Conclusion 61

Introduction

Being a teacher looks easy from the outside. It's a job everyone thinks they can do, but those who have tried it know the emotional strain it can put on a person.

It's a position so intertwined with your personality that when things aren't going well it not only feels like you're doing a bad job but that you're a useless person too.

Many teachers can't handle this and either quit or break down. The reason for this is that they haven't developed the right mindsets.

And that's what this little book is about.

The 7 Mindsets of Highly Effective Teachers will show you how to develop the emotional resilience required to be a teacher.

It's for teachers who take things too personally and allow the job to negatively impact their life. It's for teachers who are tired of beating themselves up after a bad class. It's for teachers who want to teach and live in a saner way!

This book is also a great resource for teachers just starting out. In fact, that's one of the reasons I wrote it. I wish I'd been given this book when I first began to teach because it would have prevented much of the soul-destroying self-criticism that makes the job harder than it needs to be.

I know this because I'm a teacher (no surprises there) and have taught English in Europe and Asia for many years. I've worked with students of all ages, from toddlers to adults. This has given me a unique insight into the minds of learners and what works in the classroom.

More recently I've been working at universities, where I teach students who are planning to become teachers when they graduate. I use the ideas I'm about to share in this book with them every day.

I'm not here to present myself as a perfect teacher. Although I teach the mindsets in this book I still slip out of them from time to time. That said, I discovered them while teaching and when I'm at my best I adopt them automatically anyway.

While I was writing this book some people asked what it was for. My reply was always the same – it's a personal development book for teachers. And that's exactly what it is.

Teaching is a great profession for personal development and can help us to discover a huge amount about ourselves. It's a doorway to a better understanding of who we are, because it exposes our flaws and forces us to look at the parts of ourselves we've been avoiding.

My only piece of advice for reading this book is that you need to complete the exercises. If you don't, then you probably won't get much from it. There's a huge difference between accepting what you're reading on an intellectual level and actually taking action.

Teachers who completed the exercises have told me they are now much more confident and don't allow the emotional nature of the job to get them down. If you do the same, then you too will see great changes in both your classes and your life.

So don't be the kind of teacher who complains about the difficulties of the job but never does anything to improve their own skillset. Do something about it now! Take control of your mindsets today and make teaching the inspiring and enjoyable job you know it can be.

Mindset 1

Students mirror the energy you transmit

This mindset is the foundation for all of the others, and because it's so important I'd like to begin by clarifying what I mean by energy.

When I talk about energy I'm not pointing to anything spiritual. Instead I'm referring to your dominant attitude, for example, positive, negative, relaxed or anxious. This is an important distinction because many people hear the word energy and dismiss it as woo woo.

Now you know that I'm not talking about spiritual frequencies and chakras, let me explain what I mean by students mirroring the energy you transmit.

This idea first revealed itself to me when I began to teach a class of six-year-olds in China. Before then I hadn't spent much time around children. I had no idea what to expect or how to get the best out of them so for the first few months I didn't know what I was doing.

The only good thing I can say about those classes is that at least there were no adults to witness the chaos I was spearheading.

My 'students' spent more time crawling around on the floor than in their chairs. Barely ten minutes went by without one of them crying. I couldn't connect with them at any level and every minute felt like an hour.

At the end of each class, I'd thank the Lord that I didn't have to see them for another seven days. Then the anxiety grew throughout the week as the next class edged closer.

A month into term I was in the staff room with the usual knot in my stomach when I realized I couldn't take it anymore. Teaching children was too difficult, too stressful and too awful.

While I was in this depressed state another thought arrived: "Well, it can't get any worse so you might as well just stop caring altogether."

And that's exactly what I did.

When I walked into class that afternoon it felt like a huge weight had been lifted off my shoulders. As I took the attendance roll I looked at the children and thought: "They're quite sweet when they're not crying or screaming. Who cares what happens? Life's not so bad!"

And guess what? For the next two hours I had the Midas touch.

When Jon jumped out of his chair I twirled him around until he was so tired he begged to sit back down. When Ana refused to play a game I invented a new one on the spot instead. When Nicky drew on his hands instead of in his book (again) I joked about whether he was saving his book for something special.

The class was fun, full of energy and the kids were eager to learn. It wasn't like they had magically transformed into model students overnight. The only thing that had changed was my attitude.

I'm not saying I no longer cared about the kids and had decided not to bother teaching them anything anymore. Instead my mode of thinking had changed to: "I'm going to do my best, have fun and not worry too much."

This new approach meant the kids didn't care anymore either – not in an anarchic, anything goes kind of way – but in an easy, carefree and happy way.

All of a sudden everything became clear. In previous classes the kids had been anxious because *I* had been anxious. I had received exactly what I was putting into those classes - anxiety and frustration. The moment I stopped caring I began to receive something different in return.

The lesson was clear; if you transmit anxiety you will get anxiety back. If you transmit happiness and positivity people will give that back to you instead.

Shortly after this realization I conducted an experiment to check whether it was true. The rules were straightforward – for the next week I'd enter all of my interactions with a depressed energy and see how people responded.

I soon realized that no matter how happy a person was, this changed after spending several minutes in my company. If they were very positive to begin with it took longer for them to be affected and the change wasn't so drastic. But there was still a change all the same.

A few days later I reversed the experiment - this time with the aim of being as positive and carefree as possible. I noticed that people's mood improved as they began to mirror my positive energy. At first this was only evident from their tone of voice, but soon what they were saying became more positive too.

I'm not a scientist or a psychologist. I can only offer my own experience as a teacher and in that field I've seen students mirror a teacher's energy time and time again.

However, this information will not help you to change anything if you don't figure out some ways to change your state before class. One way to do this that's worked for me is using power poses.

Power poses were developed by the social psychologist Amy Cuddy. The theory is that the body impacts the mind, so if your body is crumpled and defeated this will send a message to your brain that you feel crumpled and defeated.

The good news is that you can short-circuit this process by consciously putting your body into new positions and sending positive messages to the brain.

For example, if you want to feel powerful, strong and energetic spend two minutes with your arms outstretched as if you've just won an Olympic gold medal before class (this is particularly useful for teachers who feel powerless and exposed in the classroom).

The good thing about this is that you're not faking anything. You're going beyond conscious thought and embodying the feeling of power, which makes it real. This distinction is important because you don't want to become a person who tries to convince yourself you're fine when you're not. That's not healthy either.

But it is healthy to recognize the role your own mindset plays in class, because when you know that people mirror the energy you transmit your attitude takes on a greater importance than ever before.

Teacher's homework

I'd like you to experiment with different ways of getting into the right "state" before teaching. Don't leave it to chance. Take deliberate action to control how you feel when you walk into class.

Once you realize that you're sabotaging yourself with the energy you bring into class it's just a case of finding a method that works for you. Some things you might like to try are:

- Print out positive feedback from past student evaluations, then read this feedback to yourself before each class. This will remind you of your good qualities, guard against negativity and put you in a more positive state.

- Check out the work of Amy Cuddy and try her power poses before class. Just make sure you find somewhere private to do this (a bathroom cubicle perhaps) or risk everyone in the staff room thinking there's something wrong with you!

- Look at a photograph of yourself from when you first decided to be a teacher.

Put yourself in the shoes of this person and remember your reasons for getting into teaching in the first place. As you look at the photograph and think back to that time, try to feel the emotions you're experiencing in your body.

- If you're really pushed for time, try a few jumping jacks. Studies show that just thirty seconds of intense exercise can elevate your mood, and if nothing else you'll get a bit fitter too!

In this chapter I've discussed the impact our energy can have on other people and why taking control of our own state is so important. Next I'd like to show you how a better understanding of the way the world works can limit negativity in the classroom.

Mindset 2

Everything changes from moment to moment

We now know that our energy can have a huge impact on how students behave. But it's also important to realize that our emotions and our students' emotions are not solid things. Like everything in life they are constantly changing from moment to moment.

The best way to understand this is by studying the behavior of children, because you can tell exactly how they're feeling all of the time. If they're happy they laugh, if they're unhappy they cry and if they're angry they scream.

When I was teaching children it wasn't their laughing or screaming that surprised me but the speed at which their emotions changed. A child could be laughing one minute, crying the next and laughing again a minute later.

As adults we still experience these fluctuating emotions but we've learned to stifle them.

How does this relate to becoming a better teacher? Well, for a start it can help us to see our classes in a more positive light.

When we remember one class as "good" and another as "bad" our mind is using a shortcut to label an indiscriminate lump of time. We've taken our main memory of a class and called the whole thing "bad", forgetting about all the positive moments that happened in between.

The truth is that each hour is made up of a million moments where we experience joy, boredom, embarrassment, happiness and so on. But we tend to isolate the strongest emotion or the event that had the biggest impact and label that period accordingly.

This idea of constant change is important, because if we understand that things are changing all the time then those moments when we don't get what we want lose their heaviness. Also, by not dwelling on past moments we allow ourselves to experience the next moment instead.

This is important in terms of our relationship with our students because our minds try to simplify the way we see our students by organizing them into solid blocks.

Try this right now. Make a list of some of your current students. Now write down all the words you'd use to describe them.

Look at your list again. Does your description of these students reflect everything about them?

Of course not. And yet we carry these lists around in our heads all the time. We're constantly pigeon holing people to make life easier for ourselves.

The other day I was talking to a friend of mine. She said that every time she sees one of her co-workers it just so happens that she's in a bad mood.

Now her colleague thinks she's a negative and moody person. This is not true but now that it's solidified in the colleague's mind it may be very difficult to change his opinion.

We like to build shortcuts and we enjoy it when things conform to the shortcuts we've created. In fact, we like shortcuts so much that if something arrives to contradict them we try damn hard to reject it to maintain the status quo.

Have you ever tried to change something in your life: a habit or a personality trait perhaps? Did you notice how some of your friends didn't like it? Did you see how they pulled you up on it, told you you're not like that, and tried to force you back to where you were before?

This is exactly the same thing. Your friends are seeking out the status quo they've created in their minds and are doing whatever it takes to maintain it.

Imagine how different things would be if we saw that our students don't always conform to our perceptions. They're constantly producing behaviors we don't associate with them but we miss this because we're so wrapped up in our pre-conceived opinions.

Another way we conceal the reality that everything is changing from moment to moment is through the stories we tell ourselves. Our minds create a constant mental commentary over what's happening all the time. Often this is so noisy it takes precedence over everything else.

A good example of this is when we feel like "everything is going wrong" in a class. Suddenly we're looking for the negatives everywhere, we're telling ourselves negative stories about our teaching ability and about the students. We believe in that story rather than the truth of what's happening around us.

I experienced this when I was teaching at a Chinese university. You may be surprised to hear that it's common for Chinese students to sleep in class. Chinese children spend pretty much every waking hour at school so they learn from an early age to sleep with their heads on their desks.

I had one student who'd plug her heated pillow into the socket at the front of the classroom, collect it after I'd called attendance, then plonk it on her desk and sleep until the bell went.

During my lessons the sleeping students were all I could think about. This class is pointless, I'd tell myself. They don't want to be here; all they care about is their attendance. This story seeped into my bones and I found it hard to hide my irritation.

One day I decided to stop waking the students up (which was met with outrage as if *I'd* done something wrong) and decided to focus on the positive things happening instead.

It took me about two minutes to realize that there was actually a lot to smile about. The students in the front rows were attentive, interested and keen to learn. This came as a shock, because before that all I'd seen were the sleeping students at the back.

This simple shift in focus from the students who wanted to sleep to those who wanted to learn made a huge difference. Now I was telling myself a new story: "There are some students here who want to sleep but others are keen to learn."

After this the class became much more enjoyable. I was more positive, the students reflected this back to me, and the atmosphere changed.

Usually the stories we tell ourselves are just a series of judgements. We tend to judge moments and then those judgements become a reality for us. This stops us from fully experiencing anything.

Another way we miss the present moment is by analyzing moments that have already been and gone.

For example, perhaps a student is misbehaving in class. The teacher tries everything to get him or her to behave but it doesn't work. Eventually he loses his patience and shouts at the student. The student looks shocked and upset and goes back to work.

Five minutes later the teacher is still ruminating over the action he took. He's asking himself whether he reacted in the right way. He's feeling guilty. He's cursing the student for forcing him to become a disciplinarian rather than the inspiring and friendly teacher he wants to be.

By constantly analyzing what happened earlier the teacher misses the moment that is happening now. This means he unintentionally blocks the flow of new moments from occurring, so the class feels stale.

This idea of letting go of past moments reminds me of an old Zen tale. Two monks were travelling together through the hills of India. One morning they came to a river with a very strong current. A young woman was struggling to get across it and she asked if the monks could help her.

Both monks had taken a vow not to touch women, but the older monk picked up the woman and carried her to the other side. The younger monk was surprised by what his friend had done, but he didn't know what to say about it. So they spent the rest of the day walking in silence.

That night the younger monk didn't get much sleep. He tossed and turned, thinking about what his friend had done. By the morning he couldn't take it anymore: "We're monks!" he said, "We're not allowed to touch women! So how could you carry that woman across the river like that? "

The older monk smiled and replied: "Brother, I set her down on the other side of the river. Why are you still carrying her?"

And that's exactly what we do in class. We haul our mental baggage from one moment to the next rather than letting go and allowing space for the next moment to occur.

Teacher's homework:

In this chapter I've discussed how everything is constantly changing. This is a universal law and forgetting it will trip you up in class.

That said, this idea won't help you if you only understand it at an intellectual level. You need to be in the moment to allow the free-flow of moments to occur.

The best way to do this is through a meditation practice. When you're able to watch your own thoughts rather than being caught up in them you won't be blinded by your judgments and will see reality more clearly.

Meditation needn't be long or arduous. Just start with five minutes each morning and take it from there. Here are some basic instructions:

Sit down in a comfortable position and close your eyes.

Focus on the breath flowing in and out of your nostrils.

Don't try to manipulate the breath, just observe it flowing in and out.

You'll be shocked at how often your thoughts intervene and you forget about the task at hand.

Recognize that your mind has wandered off and, without judging this as good or bad, return to watching the flow of your breath coming in and out of your nose.

That's all there is to it, it really is that simple!

Over time you'll become more present and begin to notice the judgements you're making in class. If you catch yourself making judgements or telling yourself stories, focus on the breath flowing in and out of your nostrils. This will bring you back into the present moment again.

When I realize that I'm focusing on the negatives in class I also like to quickly find three positive things that are happening. But even recognizing that you're focusing on the negatives requires presence because otherwise you're too caught up in your own thoughts to realize you're making negative assumptions. Your meditation practice will help with this too.

Now I'm going to develop the idea of staying present and positive by talking about <u>why</u> you beat yourself up after a bad class. Imagine how great it would be if you stopped doing that forever. Well, it's possible and that's what we'll be discussing in the next chapter.

Mindset 3

It's not all about me

In the first chapter I discussed the importance of bringing the right energy to class. Once you've done this it is vital that you let go of the outcome. Otherwise you risk falling into the trap of taking everything personally and forgetting to acknowledge that there are external factors involved too. Let me give you an example.

When I first started teaching I'd get really frustrated if a class didn't go well. I'd spend hours beating myself up about what a useless teacher I was and how boring my lessons were. Eventually, two experiences put an end to this ugly habit.

The first was when I was teaching the same course to six university classes each week. I used the same material in each lesson, but some classes responded well and others showed no interest at all. I was doing the same things in each class yet the responses were poles apart.

The obvious conclusion was that how the class went wasn't only dependent on me.

I was reminded of this again while teaching a twelve-year-old in a one-to-one class. He was very intelligent, but for some reason he was always disinterested and couldn't wait to leave. After several weeks I'd had enough.

"Why do you hate these classes so much?" I asked him. "I try to make them fun but you're not interested. It's a shame because you have great potential and you could progress very quickly if you tried."

The boy shuffled in his seat. "I'm sorry, but I've been busy at school all week. Today is Saturday and I've already had three other classes this morning. I always come straight here from music class and there's no time for lunch. So I'm always tired in this class."

His schedule was surprising, but more shocking was my lack of empathy. I'd been so pre-occupied with my own performance that I'd never considered his circumstances at all.

People bring a million factors to each interaction; their past experiences, their emotions, their circumstances, or even whether they've eaten lunch. It may feel like we're failing because we're not getting the outcome we want, but in reality our own performance is just one piece of the puzzle.

No one cares about what we're doing as much as we do. But because we've spent a lot of time planning the class and now we're at the front of a room with a bunch of people looking at us we forget this. Basically, we lose perspective.

Whenever this happens to me I think back to my own schoolmates and schooldays and ask myself these questions:

Were there classes where we misbehaved because we were in a bad mood?

Yes.

Did this have anything to do with the teacher?

No.

Did our teachers make any mistakes?

Probably, but I never noticed. I was too busy trying not to look stupid, thinking about what I was going to eat for lunch and daydreaming about the weekend.

Sure, some teachers were more competent than others, but on the whole we just went to class, accepted that the teacher knew what he or she was doing and got on with it.

Unfortunately, when we transition from being students to teachers we forget that the students aren't thinking about us as much as we think they are

A former colleague of mine always struggled with this. "It's infuriating," he'd say. "I spend hours planning these classes and then I go in there and the students don't give a damn! It's as if they don't even care about the effort I've put in!"

It's not that they don't care, it's just they don't think about it. If you've never taught before why would you? When I was at school it never crossed my mind that the teachers had spent time preparing the lessons.

If you think your students lack empathy for you then you need to realize that this works both ways. How much do you focus on your own performance and how much do you empathize with your students?

If you increase your empathy for your students your classes will run much more smoothly.

Student presentations are a good time to work on your empathy. When a student gets up to present, sit down in their seat. Now think about how comfortable or uncomfortable the chair is, how hot the room is, notice how difficult it is to concentrate when someone is talking (even if what they're saying is interesting!) When the presenter asks a question, notice how you feel – do you want to answer or would you rather someone else answered instead?

You'll be amazed at how quickly you're transported into the mind of a student. You'll also realize that what's going through your mind has very little to do with the person speaking.

Another way to familiarize yourself with how it feels to be a student is by attending a part-time course. I recently completed some additional teacher training in which I was thrust back into the role of a student again. I was shocked by how often I lost concentration and at how nervous I felt when the teacher asked me a direct question. As I'm a teacher I had a degree of empathy for the instructor but this didn't change my behavior. Yes, I felt guilty when no one answered a question but this didn't override the quiet defensiveness of my "student brain."

If you make a habit of empathizing with your students, you'll close the gap between "them" and "you." This is more beneficial than trying to get the students to empathize with you (because that's probably never going to happen).

Great teachers look for ways to connect with their students because they know that once you have that connection everything becomes easier. You don't need to force knowledge onto the students because you've opened up a space where they're receptive to learning.

True connection occurs when realities merge. But because we're all so wrapped up in our own realities and focused on our own behavior this is rare.

I saw a good example of this when I was training to become a teacher. As part of the training we observed each other's practice classes and gave feedback on the teacher's performance.

One of my classmates always seemed cool and relaxed while teaching. His controlled manner made the students feel comfortable and engaged. But whenever the instructor asked how he felt the class went he only focused on the mistakes he'd made: "I was nervous, so I forgot to time the exercises and everything overran. My instructions were hazy and I spent too much time standing at the front of the room rather than monitoring the students. A few students were so bored I caught them yawning. I feel so embarrassed; it was such a terrible class!"

We were always shocked at how he picked up on so many negative things we hadn't noticed (and remember we were observing him more closely than any student ever would). But he was analyzing his performance even more closely and now he'd blown his "mistakes" out of all proportion.

When we told him that he'd looked calm and composed, that the students had been interested and his class was well organized, he seemed shocked. He'd been so preoccupied with self-criticism that he'd been unable to see what was right in front of his eyes. Then he saw everything the students did as a reaction to his own performance.

This is why developing empathy is so important. Without it we make things harder for ourselves by reacting to students as if everything they do has something to do with us.

If a student yawns in class your gut reaction might be – "I'm boring and my class is boring." But there are thousands of reasons why the student might be yawning – perhaps she didn't get much sleep the night before, perhaps she missed her morning coffee, perhaps the weather today doesn't suit her. Yet our first reaction is to see it as a reflection of something that we've done.

Once you realize that no one cares about your performance in class as much as you do, it will bring a newfound freedom to everything you do.

Teacher's homework:

This week I'd like you to develop more empathy with your students in order to stop taking things so personally in class. Here are three suggestions you can use to achieve this:

- Next time you're watching a student presentation remove your teacher's hat and try to get into the mind of a student. Pay attention to what you're feeling and why.

- Enroll in a part-time course as a student. This will remind you what it's like to be a student again (and you'll learn a new skill too!)

- Become aware of your own assumptions and challenge them. For example, if a student yawns and you think it's because the class is boring, ask yourself whether you're 100% sure that this is the case, or whether there may in fact be a billion other reasons for this behavior.

In this chapter I've discussed the pitfalls of taking things too personally and outlined some methods to overcome this. Now it's time to discuss a powerful force that many of us forget to use in class. It costs absolutely nothing and is available to us 24 hours a day – have you guessed what it is yet?

Mindset 4

I use the power of silence

In the last chapter I talked about developing empathy in order to stop taking things so personally. Empathy is one of the most useful and underused tools at our disposal. Another is silence.

It was my first boss in China who made me think about how I use silence in the classroom. He was one of those people who could talk to anyone about anything. I used to think: "How does he communicate so well? What's his secret?"

Then one day I had the opportunity to observe one of his classes. I was looking forward to it because I expected it to be loud, funny and entertaining. But when I sat down to watch the class it was none of those things. I'd never seen him so quiet before. He delivered his instructions using very few words, he monitored activities without speaking, and when he asked a question he often waited minutes for a response. At times I wondered whether the silence ought to be getting paid instead of him. But it was working – the students were calm, receptive and talkative.

After the class I told him there was more silence than I'd anticipated. He laughed and replied: "The more a teacher speaks, the more chance there is of confusing the students. You need to keep things simple and to the point. Say what you want to say and then shut up."

"That makes sense," I said, "but don't you feel awkward standing there in all that silence?

He shrugged, "To be good with people you must be comfortable with silence."

In that moment I realized that he wasn't a good communicator because he was good at talking (although he did have a lot of interesting things to say). His real skill was drawing people out by making friends with silence because it's within that silent space that true communication occurs.

Observing his class also taught me that the key to successful communication is clarity. If you use a lot of words and say a lot of unnecessary things, then your message gets lost. People only have a certain amount of concentration and if someone is just spouting words then they'll switch off.

At secondary school I had a teacher who started talking the moment the class began and barely stopped until the bell rang. He had some interesting things to say but no one listened. Some students had private conversations at the back of the room – that's how little they valued his words – it didn't matter if they missed them because more would be along in a minute.

If this teacher had allowed for more silence it would've given his words more weight. If you use silence in the right place it'll rouse peoples' interest and make them want to know what you're going to say next.

Silence is particularly effective when teaching children. This is something I realized while teaching a pair of 7-year-old Chinese twins. Their mother told me they loved dynamic activities so I made sure the classes were active. And it worked. They were in a constant state of excitement and barely realized they were learning at all.

But one day I was feeling ill so I couldn't face anything fast or physical. Instead I brought some colored pens and asked the twins to make an English calendar. Having put the equipment in front of them and told them what to do, I stopped talking. At first they looked confused that there was no game today, then they began to select their favorite colors.

A few moments later they were scratching color onto the white paper in peaceful silence. The sun drifted behind a cloud and the coolness brought more calm to the room. The twins also seemed relaxed; I could see it in their faces and in their eyes.

Then something unexpected happened; they began to ask questions. If you're not an English language teacher this won't seem like much, but I'd been working hard to get them to speak for months, so the fact they were suddenly doing it unprompted was amazing.

Whenever they asked a question I let the silence sit for a while before answering. Sometimes I wouldn't answer at all, I simply directed the question to the other twin, so there were moments when these 7-year-old children were having an English conversation.

It was a beautiful hour and I'd done nothing to create it. I'd simply walked into the room and allowed the silence to guide everything instead.

But this isn't the only advantage of allowing more silence in your classes. You can also use it to leverage tension in the room.

Like most people, I try to avoid tense atmospheres. There are two ways of doing this: physically leave the situation or find a way to break the tension. But when teaching there is a third option – use the silence to turn tension into an advantage.

This is something I discovered several years ago. Back then I was so worried about students feeling uncomfortable that I created an atmosphere where they could do no wrong. When I did get angry I hated the tension it produced so I always let students off the hook.

But, one class, that changed.

Some of my university students were giving presentations at the front of the class, the others were supposed to be listening but instead they were behaving as if they were still on their lunch break. After several warnings I lost my cool. I walked to the front of the room and yelled at them. The students had not seen me shout like this before so for a moment they were shocked. Then the silence arrived.

For the next fifteen minutes the atmosphere was tense. A fog of anxiousness hung in the air, but I was so angry I refused to release the tension. Ten minutes passed, then twenty minutes, and the atmosphere remained.

Although the atmosphere was tense the students were working hard – in fact they were working harder than I'd ever seen them work before. After half an hour I wasn't angry anymore but I decided not to release the tension because it'd be a shame to puncture the industrious atmosphere.

Occasionally a student attempted to lighten the mood by doing or saying something funny but I remained unmoved. For the remainder of the class they were on edge, but they were also attentive and engaged.

That day I realized that most people cannot handle silence. So if your tolerance for it is higher than the students then you can use this to your advantage.

My favorite teacher at secondary school provides a good example of how to use this information. She wasn't the kind of teacher who stamped her feet and bawled at students. If a student misbehaved she stopped what she was doing and stared him or her dead in the eye. The silence, combined with her unwavering eye contact, made the student so uncomfortable that he or she quickly went back to work.

This technique worked because she was more comfortable with the silence than the students. She knew that not many people can handle it when a room is quiet and someone is staring you in the eye.

If you want proof that people can't tolerate silence just look at the way they avoid silence in their interactions. Most people think they have to react to the other person with affirming grunts. Then they barely wait for the other person to finish speaking before jumping in with their own point of view. I'm not saying there's anything wrong with these people, I'm just pointing out that if they realized the power of silence it would have an incredible impact on their interactions.

Teacher's homework:

I once had a boss who talked a lot about the importance of developing presence in the classroom. He said that one way to do this was to take up space.

"Don't get stuck at the front of the classroom," he'd tell us. "As soon as you get into the classroom move around the room. Show the students you're not going to be some blurry figure at the front who they occasionally glance up at."

Taking up physical space is effective, but personally I've found that using silence is a better way to develop a strong, tangible presence.

With that in mind here are some things I'd like you try this week.

- When you enter the class, don't start talking right away. Take your time, move to the front of the class and become still first.

- Before you start talking take a few moments to look around the room. Never start talking while students are talking. Look at them and wait for them to finish instead.

- If you ask a question and no-one answers don't take the easy option and break the tension by filling the silence. Instead stay strong and wait for someone to answer.

- If you're speaking don't be afraid to leave pauses – it'll be much easier to listen to you that way.

- If a student misbehaves don't shout at them. Stop what you're doing and look them in the eyes. Wait for them to break eye contact, allow another few moments of silence and then return to what you were doing before.

The cumulative effect of bringing more silence in to your classes is huge. Students will listen to you more and they'll have more space to process what they're learning.

In the next chapter I'm going to talk about the importance of having a clear vision of how you want your classes to look, as well as how to bring more spontaneity into them. This magical combination will make boring classes a thing of the past.

Mindset 5

I am flexible

There is some truth to the maxim "if you fail to plan you plan to fail." But if your plan is too rigid then you're just as unlikely to get the results you want.

When I started teaching I didn't deviate from my lesson plan for even a second. I had worked hard on it and I was going to use it. But one afternoon I was forced to change when sixty university students raced through all my material in thirty minutes, which meant I had half an hour to fill and no ideas left.

"Right," I said, "You've finished the material more quickly than I anticipated. I can't let you go early so now I'm not sure what to do."

There was surprised laughter. Then a student raised her hand, "Why don't you tell us something about England?"

"Ok," I replied, "What do you want to know?"

"Oh I don't know, anything!"

So I began to talk.

Even at the time I didn't know what I was talking about so there's no way I can remember what I said now. And yet this class, who were famous for not paying attention, were actually listening for once. This turned into a discussion in which we addressed more language points than I ever would have covered with a lesson plan.

After that I never approached classes in the same way again. Yes, I continued to plan but I also encouraged interruptions, questions and tangents. This brought a new energy to my classes because I was responding to what was happening rather than worrying about "how things should be".

Flexibility creates a space for connection, which will bring you closer to what you want than hours of planning ever could. Students can always tell when you're religiously following a plan. In order to engage them you need to be in the moment instead.

Let's look at it another way. Before you meet a close friend do you plan exactly what you'll say and how you'll behave? Of course not. You trust the relationship enough to know that planning isn't necessary. All you have to do is turn up and see what happens.

Don't get me wrong, I'm not advocating turning up to classes with no plan at all. That's a recipe for disaster. My point is that there is a sweet spot between organization and flexibility.

I look at my lesson plan before class and pinpoint the learning goals I must accomplish. The rest of the plan is negotiable, which means I'm not worrying about cramming everything that's in my plan into the class.

When I look back to my own school days the best teachers were flexible enough to respond to things as they came up in class. For example, I had a very popular philosophy teacher at my secondary school. He listened to his students and wanted to hear their opinions. If a student raised a question he deviated from his original plan to explore it in detail.

To the untrained eye it may have looked like he was turning up without a plan. But this wasn't the case. He combined flexibility with organization and all of our discussions were related to the upcoming exams.

On the other hand, we had a French teacher who always followed a set routine. He was strict and there was no flexibility, which made the atmosphere very heavy. I always felt his was an awful model for education because we all hated the classes and were put off from learning French forever.

For me, teaching is not about doling out information like the dinner ladies dole out lunch. It's about generating interest and then allowing students to explore their own ideas. Of course there are classes where that doesn't happen, but I like to keep this at the forefront of my mind so I know what I'm aiming for. Because if you don't know what you're aiming for how will you know when you get it?

It's important to have a clear vision of what you want your classes to look like. Once you've decided on this you can use visualization to bring it into fruition. This involves visualizing your perfect class with you teaching in the perfect way.

If you're not familiar with visualization you may be skeptical. I felt the same way until a friend explained that visualizing isn't about imagining what's going to happen then crossing your fingers and hoping for it to arrive. Instead it's a way of giving your mind the opportunity to see the outcomes that you're seeking. Our brains are sophisticated machines, if we tell them what we want then eventually our subconscious will find a way to get it.

Having a clear sense of what you want will give you the confidence to be more flexible in class because you'll focus on the bigger picture rather than the details.

Teacher's homework:

Most people don't <u>get</u> what they want because they don't know <u>what</u> they want. So first you need to decide how you want your classes to look and what kind of teacher you want to be. Don't imagine you're someone else, but visualize the best version of yourself.

Now you can move onto the visualization itself. The best time to do this is early in the morning or immediately before class.

Find a quiet place and sit down.

Now close your eyes and imagine yourself as the strong, flexible and connected teacher you wish to be.

See yourself interacting with your students in the way you want to, see them looking interesting and engaged.

See yourself enjoying your job and feeling inspired.

Push yourself to imagine your perfect class in as much as detail as possible.

When I first started using this technique I noticed that much of what I was visualizing had already been happening in my classes anyway. But as I didn't know my ideal outcome I hadn't paid these things much attention or given them the credit they deserved. If you've never considered how you want your classes to look before, you may be in for a nice surprise.

In the next chapter I'm going to talk about how to get students onside. This is crucial if you want to be an effective teacher and all it takes to achieve it is a simple shift in mindset.

Mindset 6

People like you when you like them

Once you've decided: "This is a bad class and I don't like teaching these students" the class usually goes from bad to worse. Students can feel it when you don't like them and they'll begin to dislike you too. This becomes a self-perpetuating cycle and will cause more and more problems.

In order to connect with the students many teachers try to get them to like and respect them. If this is your goal, then you might like to consider that the only thing you need to change is your attitude towards them.

In the past I have worked with teachers who've used various techniques to get students onside. But in my opinion the only one who had discovered the real secret was a Chinese professor who had a fantastic reputation among the students. You just had to mention his name and their faces lit up with pleasure.

I always wondered how he did it, and one morning he invited me into his office and I had the opportunity to find out.

While he made some tea I scoured his bookshelf for the magic text on how to make students like you. There wasn't one so I studied the man himself instead. He was well dressed and quiet, if I were looking for an adjective to describe him "ordinary" would be more accurate than "charismatic."

Fed up of searching for clues I came right out with it instead. "Your students are always telling me what an amazing teacher you are and how much they like your classes."

"Are they?"

"Yes, they are. And I'm hoping you can give me some advice about how you do it."

"How I do what?"

"Get them interested, get them to listen, get them to like you."

He smiled and sipped his tea. "I don't *get* them to do anything. I like my students and I want to do my best for them. I only prepare things that will be useful to their lives. It's more work but it's worth it. Many of their classes are a waste of time, the teachers know it and the students know it. I don't want to waste my time or theirs so I teach them as if I were teaching my own children. Perhaps that's why they like me."

Once he'd said it, it was so obvious. You can't make people like you. Some people will like a person and others won't, but one thing we all have in common is that we all like to be liked!

If you don't believe me try this experiment. Next time you meet someone, forget about your own behavior and focus on the person in front of you instead. Look for things you admire about them, it needn't be anything big or spectacular; it could be something as inconsequential as the color of their shoes. Keep finding things you like about them and when you think you've exhausted the list keep going.

As you're doing this, your body language will change. When you dislike someone you tense up, but when you like them you relax. If you focus on the things you admire about a person they'll be able to sense you like them from your body language.

You'll be surprised by what a difference this makes, but this alone is not enough to ensure the person knows you like them. So it's important to use genuine compliments as well. When you focus on a person's positive traits this becomes quite easy, you'll have a handful of compliments ready to go and it's just a case of choosing one to give them.

This isn't about complimenting people just so they like you back. It's about developing your love for other people by consciously picking up on their good points. You're not doing anything dishonest. If anything you're being more honest because most people skew reality by focusing only on the negatives.

I first realized how powerful compliments can be while teaching at a vocational college in China. It was midwinter, freezing cold, and the facilities were dreadful. There was no heating and because the windows didn't close it felt like we were outside. I was wearing a hat, coat, scarf, gloves and several pairs of socks. My students were wearing what looked like every item of clothing they owned. It was impossible to think of anything apart from the cold.

Halfway through the class a sense of defeat hung in the air. This was nothing new. These students had got poor scores in their university entrance exams, which is why they'd finished up at a vocational college. Now their parents liked to remind them that their lives probably weren't going to amount to much.

It was sad and I felt sorry for them, but if their effort level in my classes was anything to go by it's no wonder they performed so poorly at school.

I'd nominated a girl at the back of the room to read aloud. After looking at me as if she was going to kill me she plodded through the text with zero enthusiasm and a million inaccuracies. Eventually her voice faded into the background and I became aware of how I was correcting her instead.

"No, stop there. It's 'the' not 'de'. Ok, go on. No! It says hypocrisy. We did that last week! Go on, no, you've missed a word, go back."

My voice reminded me of something I'd seen in a park a few weeks earlier. I was walking past a kids' football game when I noticed a father running up and down the line shouting instructions at his son. This made the child nervous, so he kept making mistakes. This infuriated the father who shouted at him for being useless. I remember thinking that the child would be better off if his father didn't have a mouth and could only clap instead.

Yet now, in this freezing classroom, I was doing exactly the same thing as him. I was so disgusted with myself that for the rest of the class I decided to only praise the students instead.

When the girl finished reading I said: "I was only correcting you because you have so much potential and I want to see you improve."

She blushed, sat down, and looked so moved I thought she might cry.

After that I drilled some words with the class (Chinese students enjoy this for some reason). When we'd finished, I told them that their pronunciation was improving week by week, which was true, and that they ought to be proud of themselves. When I said this I literally felt the energy change in the room. The bitterness disappeared and in its place came warmth.

After that the rest of the class was a joy, I'd never seen the students work so hard.

I'm not suggesting we compliment people all of the time - that would be ridiculous. I'm just saying that if we want better results we might like to consider giving genuine praise more often.

Personally, I don't just give compliments to boost students' motivation or make them like me. I do it because I find it sad that people are so negative about themselves. It's easy to forget this because a person's outward projection rarely reflects their inner insecurity. We see a person and we think they haven't got any problems, but often the opposite is true.

This is easy to forget, so I've developed a method to remind myself of it at the beginning of each class. When I enter the classroom I take a moment to look at each student with compassion. I tell myself that they're all humans and they're doing their best in the face of difficulties that I'm not aware of.

I find that it's also a good indicator of where I am in terms of my mindset on that particular day. Sometimes I'll realize that I'm in a negative state because feeling compassion for the students is difficult. On other occasions I realize how happy and hopeful I feel because I'm able to generate compassion without trying too hard. So, like all the best processes, this one inadvertently teaches you something about yourself too.

Teacher's homework:

- Challenge yourself to go a whole class without saying anything negative. Monitor whether this impacts the class in a positive or negative way. Also monitor how you feel about the class afterwards.

- Make a point of looking at your students with compassion whenever you enter a class. This will help you to connect with them and it'll also teach you about your emotional state that day.

- Whenever someone does something well in class (or anywhere for that matter) don't hold back. Tell them! It sounds so obvious, but be honest, how often do you do it?

In this chapter I've discussed the idea that students like you when you like them. But this doesn't mean pandering to the students' needs all the time because, as you're about to find out in the final chapter, this type of behavior can be dangerous.

Mindset 7

I can't please everyone all of the time

To a certain extent we all want to please people, but this affects some of us to a higher degree. From a psychological perspective people-pleasing is dangerous, because you're always putting yourself last. This means you stifle what you want and these repressed needs fester inside you.

One way of getting over this is realizing that every student needs different things, so you're never going to please them all anyway.

For example, I had a university class in China who were particularly challenging. After just fifteen minutes of the first class a girl shouted: "Boring!" Not what you want to hear when all you've done is introduce yourself.

Over the next few months this class went from bad to terrible. No matter what I did they were never satisfied. It was as if they'd decided to reject the work before they'd walked through the classroom door.

I asked my colleagues for some advice but they didn't have any: "Sometimes you get classes like that."

Eventually I asked the students what *they* wanted to do in my classes. Their response was astonishing. For every student who wanted to listen to English music, another thought this was pointless. For every student who wanted to learn about British culture, another wanted to focus on grammar. No two students could agree on anything; trying to please them all at once was impossible.

Let's question for a moment where our need to please people comes from. The answer often stems from our insecurities. We think we're not good enough so we attempt to boost our self-esteem by seeking praise from others. This is dangerous - we can't control the actions of others or how they feel, so we're recklessly placing our self-esteem in the hands of other people.

Yes, it's nice to be liked by your students, but needing their approval is one of the worst mindsets you can have. Some people don't even realize they're doing it so if you're aware of your tendency to people-please then congratulations, you're way ahead of most.

Trying to please everyone all of the time will have a negative impact on many areas of your class and the most obvious one is discipline.

A few weeks after I first started teaching children, the Director of Studies observed one of my regular classes. These classes had not been going well for a while and this one was no different. The kids constantly talked over me, no one listened, and at one point a child jumped out of his chair and crawled around at my feet. I was so intent on not upsetting anyone that I didn't react to any of these things.

After the class the Director of Studies gave me some feedback.

"Do you want kids crawling around at your feet?" he asked.

I thought about this for a moment.

"Well?" He repeated, "Do you?"

"No, I don't."

"Then in that case you need to show them it's unacceptable."

The strange thing was that I'd never considered how I wanted the students to behave. I'd been taking all my cues from the students rather than the other way around. If anything, trying to please them had the opposite effect: they were nervous and uncertain because I hadn't given them any boundaries. The child that crawled around on the floor wasn't pleased, he was bored and wanted attention. The others were annoyed because I allowed him to disrupt the class and get away with it. It was the epitome of poor leadership and it all stemmed from not wanting to be disliked.

I once discussed this notion of people-pleasing with an older colleague of mine. She was very popular with most students, but she was also quite strict, so she had a few detractors who really hated her.

"Doesn't it bother you that you've got students in your class that dislike you?" I asked.

She laughed, "Not really. Even Jesus wasn't liked by everyone."

I've never forgotten that response. Jesus healed people, he put others first, he turned water into wine, but did everyone like him? No. In fact, some people hated him so much they hammered him to a cross.

The fact is that some students are going to dislike you regardless of what you do. This has more to do with them than you so there is no point stressing yourself out about it.

What you can do, however, is create a list of things that you will and won't accept in the classroom. This reverses the habit of people-pleasing and you begin to play by your own rules instead.

I did this a few years ago and it's had a huge impact on my classes. To give you a better idea of what I mean, here are some of the items on my list:

- I always encourage my students.

- I have confidence in the material I have developed and its practical application.

- I create a space where students are not afraid to speak and are not criticized for their point of view.

- I do not pander to students who are not interested in the class.

- I will not tolerate students laughing at other students.

- I will not tolerate students talking over each other or talking over me.

When I first wrote this list I carried it around with me and glanced at it whenever I had a spare moment. Before long I'd memorized it.

Because I'd thought hard about why these rules were necessary I found it easy to implement them - and if students didn't like me for it then so be it.

This simple process yielded instant results; all of a sudden my classes had order and purpose. And while some of the students were annoyed by the new rules, others seemed to appreciate the clear boundaries I'd set.

The bottom line is that there'll always be people who dislike you. You need to become ok with that because the alternative is watering yourself down to the extent that you're neither loved nor hated by anyone. Winston Churchill summed it up best when he said: "You have enemies? Good. It means you have stood up for something, sometime in your life."

Teacher's homework:

Make a list of what you will and won't accept in class.

Now ask yourself why each point is important and write this down. If you can't think of a reason, then cross that item off the list.

Copy your list onto a new piece of paper. Remember to include your reasons for each item (this will remind you that your rules are part of a bigger vision).

Keep your list in your back pocket and glance at it whenever you can. After a week or so you shouldn't need to look at it anymore.

Making a list of rules is a quick and simple thing to do, but you'll be amazed by the clarity and order it brings to your classes. And what teacher wouldn't want that?

Conclusion

In this book I've shown you 7 mindsets that have been extremely beneficial to me as a teacher. But these aren't the ONLY mindsets out there. You're a unique person with your own way of doing things, so take some time to develop your own personal mindsets too. Figure out what works for you, because there's no catch-all manual for teaching. Just as there's no catch-all manual for life.

If you disagree with a mindset in this book that's fine, so long as you haven't written it off without testing it first. As I mentioned in the introduction, taking action is the key. It's only through doing things that we truly discover anything. It's easy to take this stuff on board intellectually but more difficult in practice (particularly for teachers who have a habit of intellectualizing things!) So if you haven't completed the exercises, go back and do them now. You'll be surprised by what you discover about your teaching and about yourself.

If you agree with the mindsets but struggle to adopt them, just remember that like everything in life this is a journey. I doubt any of us will ever get to the stage where we can say: "I'm a great teacher now. I no longer need to learn anything new."

None of us are perfect, we don't have all the answers and we shouldn't expect ourselves to. We're constantly evolving and learning, because we may be teachers but like everyone else we're students of life too.